Our Numbered Days

Our Numbered Days

Neil Hilborn

Button Poetry / Exploding Pinecone Press
Minneapolis, Minnesota
2015

Published by Button Poetry / Exploding Pinecone Press
Minneapolis, MN 55403

http://buttonpoetry.com

Cover Design: Doug Paul Case || dougpaulcase@gmail.com

ISBN 978-0-9896415-6-2

Table of Contents

Our Numbered Days	3
MSP PHI LGA ALB PHI MSP	5
Ballad of the Bruised Lung	6
Joey	7
Our Numbered Days	9
Snow Theory	10
Unsolicited Advice to Minnesota Children	11
Fabric Swatches, Paint Samples	12
Bystander Paralysis	13
Not Dead	14
All Harvestmen Are Missing a Leg	16
Memorial Day	17
Future Tense	18
April, 2013	20
Our Numbered Days	21
Chitin	23
The Sadness Factory	24
Ekphrasis with Peeled Onions	26
Phreaking	27
The Talk Show Host Has a Nosebleed on National Television	29
The New Sheets	30
Again	31
Our Numbered Days	32
You Can Look	33

This Machine Kills Fascists 35

Dust Mop 36

Song for Paula Deen 37

OCD 38

What the Cicadas Don't Understand 41

Moving Day 42

Little Poems 43

Parking Meter Theory 46

Skyline with Cranes and Stormcloud 47

Our Numbered Days 48

On Sitting on My Ex-Girlfriend's Porch, Listening
 to Her Play a Song about Me that I Know
 Her New Boyfriend Helped Her Write 49

I'm Sorry Your Kids Are Such Little Shits
 and that We Are in the Same Zen Garden 50

The News Anchor Is Crying 51

Our Numbered Days 52

Here and Away 53

Our Numbered Days 55

Traffic, Lightning, Gutter 56

Enabling: a Love Song 57

American Revolution Trail, Charlotte,
 North Carolina, Winter 59

It Was the Day I First Fell out of a Window... 60

Liminality 61

Our Numbered Days

The best way to get to heaven is to take it with you.
Henry Drummond

Heaven isn't a place, it's a feeling.
Sierra DeMulder

Heaven will be no heaven to me if I do not meet my wife there.
Andrew Jackson

In many languages, the word for heaven is the same as the word for sky.
Wikipedia

I will sing to you all the things I stopped myself from saying while we were alive.
the author

All the way to heaven is heaven.
St. Catherine of Siena

I hope the exit is joyful and I hope never to return.
Frida Kahlo

The light dimmed, and the singing in his head stopped.
Louise Erdrich

When my mother dies, I will lead her
like a dog into the space between
our walls which is just like the space
between here and always, the king
and the kingdom. I will lead her by the hand
if she be blind and I will wag my tail
against her knees if she be afraid
and I will leave her at the gate.

Life on earth will in some ways
be easier. I will not have to return
her phone calls. I will not have to feel
guilty when I want to hear no more
no more about the divorce. I won't cry

3

though I will want to cry. Though I will hate myself
for not crying. When my mother dies,
if I am still alive, I will slouch
on my knees as though in prayer, I will
write one or two poems, then I will
no longer think of her.

MSP PHI LGA ALB PHI MSP

How miraculous that we all
keep our shit together. How miraculous
that no one has a premonition of flames
and tries to open the cabin door. The airline
pilot next to me keeps his eyes closed
during takeoff and landing. He does not
drink anything. I have an orange juice
with no ice. I want to watch the horizon
as it gets farther away. This man
might just be smarter than me, but he is also
flying coach and reading the sports section
while I do crosswords, so he is probably
still smarter than me. Pretension
can look like intelligence if you squint
hard enough or wear glasses. There are,
for some reason, always Buddhist monks
in the Philadelphia airport. Buddhist monks
rewrapping their robes. This is my sixth time
in this airport. My sixth time because of two
different women. I have paid probably
a couple thousand dollars for the privilege.
Five cheesesteaks. Surprisingly good caramel
popcorn. Maybe thirty hours, five just trying
to find outlets. How miraculous that I can go
basically anywhere. How miraculous, the doors,
the wings, the recycled air. How miraculous,
flight is just a fall that never finds the ground.

Ballad of the Bruised Lung

Many things happen in your life that shouldn't:
the black spot that grew into cancer, the subcompact

that just could not wait to meet you; maybe things do
happen for a reason but that reason is stupid. Maybe

your brother fell out of a window only because
he's an asshole. I love you, but I can't keep

letting you show up where I am and remind me
of what I said to you all those times

I was drunk that one time. Most of them were just
hurtful nonsense, but I am proud of "You are like

a comet: every so often you come around
to fuck up my shit." In a perfect world, all the towns

in Illinois would be named "Blood" so I could
no longer pick out yours on a map. When you're dumb

enough for long enough, you're gonna meet someone
too smart to love you, and they're gonna love you

anyway, and it's gonna go so poorly. It must be
odd for our mutual friends who like me more

but think you were right. To say I hate you would imply
a world in which I kissed more than your stomach. Look,

we've established that I'm a jerk, so let me say this:
I am a flat tire and you are a pothole full of lug nuts.

I am a pile of bricks and you are holding a sledgehammer,
which is to say I would not exist without you.

Joey

Joey always told me, laughing, as though
it were actually a joke, that he wanted
to kill himself but it was never the right

time. There were always groceries
to be bought and little brothers
to be tucked in at night. Don't worry.

Joey isn't going to kill himself
twenty more lines into this poem. That's not
the kind of story I'm telling here.

Joey got a promotion and now he can
afford Prozac. Joey is Joe now. Joe
is a cold engine in which none of the parts

complain. Joe is a brick someone made
out of fossils. If you removed money
from the equation, Joey would have been painting

elk on cave walls. People would have fed him
and kept him away from high places
because goddamn, look at those elk. I think

that the genes for being an artist and mentally ill
aren't just related, they are the same
gene, but try telling that to a bill collector.

We were 17, and I drove us all to punk shows
in a station wagon older than any of us. We were
17 and I bought lunch for Joey more often

than I didn't. We were 17 and the one time Joey
tried to talk to me about being depressed
when someone else was around, I told him to

shut the hell up and asked if he needed to change
his tampon. You know that moment when the cartoon
realizes he's taken three steps off the cliff

and he takes a long look at the audience
like we are carrying the last moving box
out of a half-empty house? Joey looked like that

without the puff of smoke. He just played
video games for a half hour and then went home. Once
I found Joey in my dad's office, staring at the safe

where he knew we kept the guns. Once Joey
molded his car into the shape of a tree trunk
and refused to give a reason why. I once caught

Joey in Biology class staring at his scalpel
like he wanted to be the frog, splayed out,
wide open, so honest. There's one difference

between me and Joey. When we got arrested,
bail money was waiting for me at the station.
When I was hungry, I ate. When I wanted to

open myself up and see if there really were
bees rattling around in there, my parents got me
a therapist. I can pinpoint the session

that brought me back to the world. That session
cost seventy-five dollars. Seventy-five dollars
is two weeks of groceries. It's a month of bus fare.

It's not even a school year's worth of new shoes.
It took weeks of seventy-five dollars to get to the one
that saved my life. We both had parents that believed

us when we said we weren't OK, but mine could afford
to do something about it. I wonder how many kids
like Joey wanted to die and were unlucky enough

to actually pull it off. How many of those kids
had someone who cared about them but also
had to pay rent? I'm so lucky that right now

I'm not describing Joey's funeral. I'm so
lucky we all lived through who we were
to become who we are. I'm so lucky I'm so—lucky.

Our Numbered Days

They dreamt not of a perishable home.
William Wordsworth

July is gone like the gasoline it took to make the circle again:
Florida to Florida by way of America.
Laura Jane Grace

                    All that brooded,
ignorant in your safe arms, concluded.
Ruth Stone

Home is wherever people know our stories.
Sam Cook

The worst lie is to say good-bye.
Where are you going that I won't follow?
Calvin Forbes

Home to people like me is not a place but all places, all places
except the one we happen to be in at the moment.
Anthony Burgess

Books; china; a life
Reprehensibly perfect.
Philip Larkin

In the past ten years, I have seen
my father perhaps ten times, and while
that is almost certainly an exaggeration
it tells the truth of this story: my house
only felt like a home underwater, in floods;
my father was an astronaut because to me
stars or the distant flashing of satellites
seemed closer than wherever he was;
when I hear a Jeep outside, I think
it might be him, come to get me.

Snow Theory

When you hear the phrase Winter Weather Advisory
you imagine a guidance counselor and snow
that is unsure what it wants to do with its life,
don't you? Don't you see skills tests
about its life before it rebecomes
water? The name plate on the counselor's
desk reads Felipe Rios. Señor Rivers,
as Snow calls him, has a constant supply
of green highlighters. No one knows
how he gets them, because rivers can't walk
to the store or be guidance counselors,
duh. If snow can drift, so can leaves
and dust and responsibilities. You can have
a light dusting of feathers. Snow is a sentient being
that hates when people drive in straight lines. Snow is
migratory. Snow is a dog that wants
all the sidewalks to be covered
in salt. Snow therefore is a happy dog.
Imagine if fire extinguishers were full
of snow. Imagine the fun we could have.

Unsolicited Advice to Minnesota Children

Listen here, you little shits. You are growing
up in one of the most beautiful places
on earth. Everything here is all decked-out
elk and the imperial majesty of winter
and you ingrate children of the snow
spend all your time in "classes"
learning about "things" that will teach you
nothing about ice skating on the bones
of your enemies or lighting moose
on fire or felling fir trees
the beaver way or how to make friends
in a blizzard which is with a shovel.
What I'm saying is, it's beautiful
as a mushroom cloud out here, and by the time
your grandchildren can enjoy it, it's all going
to be a tepid ocean anyway, so whatever
you do, put some of it inside your head before
it's gone. It's all yours, you bastards. It's all yours.

Fabric Swatches, Paint Samples

As you can already see, everything is fucked.
Paul Guest

I will, in all my hereditary optimism,
try to be honest my dear, not just
about where I am and particularly
with whom, but also where I am in the vast,
melodramatic plane that is my feelings
and where I have placed you
and how exactly to cross
the Stupid Desert to find me.
There is quicksand in the Stupid
Desert that I call my exes—they don't
hate you but, my darling, they also
do not know you, which is not to say
I don't speak of you, because I do,
I do, to my therapist
who I fired, to the women
at bars and at work and
at Roller Derby bouts who confuse
me for an exit sign, darling,
I use you, yes, to feel secure or loved,
or like a tire wrapped in chains,
so let us say at least that I do not
use you abnormally. All of this
is to say that, should you move here
to live with me and the mental
disorders I call friends and mental
disorders, I will not lie to you. The sea
is so wide and our boat is so small.

Bystander Paralysis

It is, as it turns out, very difficult
to get Ikea furniture into the trunk
of a subcompact. Harder still
when you are a middle-aged woman
who I theorize does not work out (not
because she is a woman or middle-aged,
but because she is screaming "Curse
these weak, beautiful arms!") and your son,
who I guess is my age, is sitting
in the front seat staring at what I hope
is his phone. The corners of the box
are becoming quite sad. I am,
as I said, probably her son's
age. I am not helping her
because that would be like
asking her to adopt me and I already
have a mother who I don't
call enough. Maybe her son
doesn't have legs. Maybe he does
but that doesn't change the fact
that his mother is a huge jerk. I am not
helping because I have already
assumed so much, and I would rather
let her suffer than be wrong.

Not Dead

In the bar, before the lights
are on but after all the rails
are clean. In the station wagon

I learned to drive then wrecked. In
the morning, always in the morning.
In the basement of that tea shop

that, for some reason, employed
both of us. In the neighbor's yard
on Halloween. In the middle school,

high school, and community college
boiler rooms. In a snow plow,
once. I should have been saying "goodnight"

and fucking meaning it. I should have
been in my kitchen and not that kitchen
where my arms were way too long

to be arms, or in the coffee shop,
or the other goddamn coffee shop, or in
the street when it had just started

snowing. When I say I'm on my way
I probably mean it, I probably
want to die less than I say I do,

but who knows, the statistics
are sporadic at best. I'll say I love
you when I actually love you.

We are in your mother's house
and I guess I want to be here. There's no
reason not to, I guess. I guess

I'd rather be tattooing a bunch of triangles
on myself or ordering a steak
at an Indian restaurant or setting

all my shit on fire, but none of those
are currently reasonable options. If anyone
is gonna kill me, it should be me. No,

I won't kiss you, it's the wrong
season. The nearest place you can buy a gun
is only twenty minutes away. I'm not going

to tell you how to live your life, but maybe you should
listen to your feet when they tell you to run
the fuck away. Maybe you should get out of here,

then get out some more. I was trying
to take apart a clock and put it back together
before it noticed. I was trying to kiss you

and blame someone else. Kissed the sidewalk
instead of you. Kissed anyone I actually
love. It's so hard to love you

because who the fuck are you? I feel
like I've spent my whole life waiting
for this moment and now this moment

is terrible. This moment doesn't even
have any fireworks. This moment falls asleep
with its keys in its hand. It's not your fault,

probably because you didn't make me
this way, stupid, no, I mean I'm stupid, I mean
you might be stupid, who knows, who

the fuck are you, but anyway, I thought
cheating on my girlfriend would be so great, and now
that I've kissed you, all that's happened

is I've kissed you. In the pile of snow
over the pile of leaves, in your car, on the train,
always slightly hoping someone would catch me.

All Harvestmen Are Missing a Leg

All drivers in St. Paul must have
broken ankles. I have a broken ankle
and am driving like them, poorly,

therefore I declare this to be true.
The harvestman, in case you were

wondering, is that spider with the tiny
body and long legs, referred to
by the unimaginative South as a Daddy
Long Legs, though I admit it would be
funnier to imagine all people who harvest
hopping on one leg. Not funnier. Did I say

funnier? I meant somber and embarrassing.
I meant whatever doesn't offend you.
Don't ask me questions if you don't
want to hear stupid answers. I'm not good

at many things, but I have been called
the Pierre Renoir of being privileged

by absolutely no one ever. But let's not
forget about the terrible St. Paul drivers.
They're so bad that I don't go out

when it's raining. I don't go out
anyway, but that's because of the anxiety.
The anxiety comes out when it is
and isn't snowing. All snow is missing

its drivers. All drivers are missing a leg.
All legs aren't working right today. All
appointments today are being missed. All beds,
all beds today are full.

Memorial Day

The old lesbian couple is sitting
in the park overlooking St. Paul. They are
holding hands as though one or both of them

have cancer. Or maybe it is their anniversary
but their car was just towed. Or maybe
I should assume nothing about their genders

or sexual orientations because from here
they are indistinct and from here
I cannot tell. But they are holding hands

and they look like they have been crying
and the flags are all waving and people
are all walking uphill and night

is coming on and I am sitting
in this park watching an old couple almost cry
together, and I want this to be

the most important thing I do all year.

Future Tense

And when your fourth love leaves you,
you will want to kill yourself but
you won't. You no longer think of suicide
as a house you will build one day.

Your fourth love, who is your first
real love, who brought you peace
when your whole body was a gun:
when she leaves you, ask your roommate

to hide the knives because you will carve
her name into all of the food in your fridge.
Stop showering. Warmth will remind you
of her. Masturbate in public. Hope someone

catches you. You need to feel vulnerable
in front of anyone else. Try to burn her
clothes. Try to fall in love with strangers.
Try to fall asleep without her: open the windows:

she would have wanted them closed;
turn off the radio: she can't sleep without
noise—you can't sleep without noise,
but noise will sound like her whispering

you into the world of lights and breakfast;
make the rain sound like nothing, make
the rain sound nothing like her voice.
Don't be alone. When you are alone,

you won't do anything you did with her,
so you won't do anything. Marvel at how she,
the patient gardener, the bringer of sleep,
she who draws the bath and lights the candles,

she who made you someone who could make
himself into someone, she made you want
to live more than anything else, and now
she makes you want to leave the world

because you have seen it. In her
you have seen the color and shape
of your perfect life and now the children,
the house, the arguments about tablecloths,

they are all fading like things left in sunlight,
like any dream left too long in the light.
For months—years—every time you see her
you will want to kiss her. When you do,

you will expect pain to come like the old dog
you could never bring yourself to put down,
but there will be none. You will remind yourself,
she will remind you, you will remind each other,

that this is for the best, that you are physically
incapable of loving one another, and in those
moments you will be lying, your heart screaming
I CAN I CAN I CAN. But you'll stay silent.

Because of her. Because she asked for this.
Because she filled something in you
that's still full, even though
she's gone.

April, 2013

Crime rates rise with the temperature. Elsewhere
in the country, a bomb has exploded

at a marathon. A fertilizer plant has exploded
in Waco. A coffee shop has exploded in Iraq.

Many things have exploded in Syria. Where I come from,
everyone is surprised no one has flown a plane
into the refineries. I am no longer from

where I come from. I live in Minnesota,
and in Minnesota it has just snowed seven inches.
Winter forever means I will be safe

forever. We have all been stuck in our houses
for so long that we are growing used to them.

Who would build a bomb in this weather? Who
would plot anything this morning? Who would want
all our houses to be ash or hospitals or tombs

or anything other than houses? It's been so cold
for so long that my fingers could not build anything
other than a fire, but the robins, well, the robins arrived
today. The forecast calls for rain.

Our Numbered Days

You never give away your heart; you lend it from time to time.
If it were not so, how could we take it back without asking?
  Jeanette Winterson

You are always ticking inside me.
  Sierra DeMulder

I loved the way she changed before the dark did,
the woman inside of her stepping out of her jeans.
  Jason Shinder

There are two beds in the room. Of course
we make love in one, fall asleep in the other.
  Sherman Alexie

I counted out my future children's names like stars,
I let him touch my back
under my shirt.
  Eireann Lorsung

                              She made you want
to live more than anything else, and now she makes you
want to leave the world because you have seen it.
  The author

So maybe love is a form of crying.
  Catie Rosemurgy

through the gate into dusk you've gone like the day.
  Paul Guest

I have been wondering, mostly, if love
and sanity are the same thing. When I say
I am in love I am also saying the world
makes sense to me right now.

I know that love is not the same as knowing
everything, but because she is gone, because

about her there are unknowns that will now remain
unknowable, it is important to list what is mine
to list: she likes hazelnut in her coffee; she is a
better driver when the transmission

is manual; though she couldn't name it, her favorite
color is Bakelite seafoam green; she loved me once,
though it wasn't for very long, though it was
distracted, though it shouldn't have
happened, once, she loved me.

Chitin

My ex-girlfriend, for the fifth time
this morning (and when, I wonder,
does she become just my friend?),
swats my hand away

from my mouth as I chew
on my nails. She imagines my stomach
as a bird's nest of finger ends. She
imagines the digestive system

as it ought to be, karmically.
She imagines me full of dead things,
re-consuming that which
I am trying to grow out of.

She is not wrong, but I hate
telling her she is not wrong,
and really isn't this a metaphor
for shit, anyway? As in,

I am holding onto some shit.
Neil, you just have to let that
shit go. Stop biting
your nails. Let it go.

The Sadness Factory

is where I go when I run out of
Missing You. Because the door

is three feet high, you have to
crawl into the Factory. Let me tell you

about leaving: it's either the drain
or the window. The carpet

at the Sadness Factory is all shag.
The drapes? Also shag. The walls

are supposed to change color with your mood,
but they have been broken since the 80s,

which I hear were a rough time for empathic
architecture. The Sadness Factory is, no joke,

shaped like a heart. Sadness is the corniest
of emotions. The most popular time to visit

the Factory is at night because, again,
corniness, so they have hired the world's most

incompetent security guard. He is always
weeping and saying something unintelligible

about my wife, my wife. Sadness
is much easier when you are reminded,

by phone, by accident, of what makes
you happy, so the Factory always smells

like maple syrup and snowmelt. There's no
golden ticket. Iron, though. Cement. The lines

for samples are prohibitively long: New Apartment
Sadness; Everything Is Great but Something

Feels Off Sadness; A Midsummer
Night's Sadness; The Sadness of Wanting

To Break Something but Being Too Weak;
The Sadness that Comes from Always Knowing

Exactly Where You Are.

Ekphrasis with Peeled Onions

after Peeling Onions by Lilly Martin Spencer

I am not convinced those are onions.

Onions do not make you cry
like an opera singer. I have to assume,

therefore, that she is an opera singer and that

therefore the plenty around her is about to
disappear; you cannot be an artist

and also know plenty. The jars, the somehow

very ripe fruit, the gold earrings, gone.
All that's left is the knife and the onion.

The knife, barely indistinguishable from the wall,

barely for now. The way the blade stays
out of focus until it's called. The way

your life is sharper once it's gone.

Phreaking

is the act of stealing a phone call.

1. In 1968, John Draper built a small blue box
with parts so simple they might as well
have been magic. He stepped into
the California sunshine. He found two
payphones, one next to the other, and launched

his voice around the world to the payphone
next to him. He answered "Hello?"
and in the five seconds before the sound
returned to his ears, his voice unhitched itself
from his throat. "   ."

2. My girlfriend moved to California
and my cell phone is starting to replace her.
When it rings, I feel like she's touching me.
I can feel it vibrate in my pocket
even when I know it's off.

3. Still standing at the payphone, John Draper
tried to speak. He was choking on nothing. His voice
was locked somewhere out there. He sent it away
and it could not come back. He opened his mouth
and all that came out was static and the Pacific.

4. I am driving to her and somewhere in the middle
of America my car breaks down. My phone dies
in my hand. This country is closing

around me. There are so many
stars. I call out her name but it's
swallowed by all that distance.

5. In 1971, AT&T had John Draper arrested.
The police released him without charge.
How do you jail a man

just for speaking? There are no words
for the theft of time and distance.

6. When we call each other halfway
across the country, we are paying
for the illusion that space does not exist.
We are paying to pretend
that one day, if we reach hard enough,
we will touch each other.

7. That night, John Draper heard his voice
laughing at him. It was in the walls. It was
in the phone lines. He took a pickaxe and started digging.
With every swing all he could hear was HELLO HELLO HELLO.

8. When she calls me, her laugh
crackling over the Midwest,
I feel farther from her than when we

are not speaking. I reach and touch
nothing. I hear phone lines in the wind
they are calling my name.

9. John Draper had the same dream every night:
an endless field of robots with his voice; his voice
watching him sleep; his voice digging
its own grave; his voice building walls
and a roof out of wire.

10. I have not seen her in so long. To me,
she is only a ghost in a machine. She is only
a memory, like a broken flashlight
or summer. For her,

I sent away the best parts of me.
I haven't come back.

The Talk Show Host Has a Nosebleed on National Television

No, the talk show host becomes a moth. No,

she enters wearing Klan robes. No, she

interviews exclusively cartoon characters

from now on. No, she tells Mickey Rourke

to suck it. No. Bad plan. She sets

the clock back. She's a woman

with that nosebleed. The talk show

host opens the window and flies

away, she flies away.

The New Sheets

after Ross Gay

Because I love you, I shouldn't tell you this, but
I put a single red sock in with your sheets. Also,
I used the detergent with the muscular arm
and the tool instead of the bubbles and clouds. Also,
I turned the temperature knob at random
and darling, please don't take this to mean
that I think erratically of our love. Also, I tried
to use bleach but found a bottle instead
that somehow I cannot find again that somehow,
somehow, made the pink a brighter pink and darling,
I am telling you this not because you would find
out—you are absentminded and would convince
yourself you had done this to yourself,
I am telling you this because I love you,
and if anyone should hurt you, it should be me.

Again

also after Ross Gay

Because I love you, I shouldn't tell you this, but
I put a single red sock in with your sheets. Also,
I used the detergent with the muscular arm
and the tool instead of the bubbles and clouds. Also,
I turned the temperature knob at random
and darling, please don't take this to mean
that I think erratically of our love. Also, I thought
of using bleach but instead found your hair
dye, your red, red hair dye, and I poured
it in, all of it, because you were tired
of our bed, because we needed a new
washing machine anyway and darling,
I am telling you this not because you would find
out—you are absentminded and would convince
yourself you had done this to yourself,
I am telling you this because I love you,
and if anyone should hurt you, it should be me.

Our Numbered Days

Day, n. A period of twenty-four hours, mostly misspent.
Ambrose Bierce

O, call back yesterday, bid time return.
William Shakespeare

Time goes, you say? Ah no, alas, time stays, we go.
Henry Austin Dobson

Come on, skinny love, just last the year.
Justin Vernon

And what of the dead? They lie without shoes
in their stone boats. They are more like stone
than the sea would be if it stopped.
Anne Sexton

...a time to gather stones.
King Solomon

Time is making fools of us again.
Albus Dumbledore

The clock talked loud.
Tillie Olsen

What has died: lightbulbs; all of my pets; my
family; the economy and thereby
my predilection for bad art and alcohol; the part
of me that allows me to love as though
I were not falling; me in the future; me
in alternate dimensions; everything
that is not at this moment fucking: everything
that will not be; my grandmother and
my aunt; the you in my head, the me
in my head and the you and me I have
made you and me in my head. There is
never enough time.

You Can Look

This is what it's like to be in love
with two people at the same time. This is
what it's like to get drunk in a mansion. You will never

live here; don't get so comfortable. This is what
it's like to live in a house full of antiques. This is
what it's like to kiss someone until you are

no longer sorry you kissed them. These two people you
love, they are two temps doing the same job, separated only
by a cubicle wall. They are both trying

to fill a hole that wasn't empty in the first place. You keep
calling yourself empty and you're starting
to believe it. This is what it's like to smash

your friend's television. This is what it's like to set
fire to the clothes you are wearing. This is what it's like
to turn a suicide note into a paper airplane. This

is what it's like to turn a life full of exclamation marks
into a blank page. This is the day you finally reach
the cookie jar and find it full of seeds.

This is what it's like to buy the wrong kind
of flowers. This is what it's like to read your lover's
mail and find they are doing nothing wrong. Have you ever

set a field on fire and called it a birthday candle? Have you
ever punished a dog because you trained it wrong? This is
what it's like to build a wall in your living room.

This is what it's like to use bricks when you should have used
sand. The one you loved first, you only kiss her through a hole
in that wall. You describe the way your body would feel

against her hands as though you are an ancient city
she will visit one day. Every night you say it is
the last night. This is what it's like to sell your shoes

in the desert. This is what it's like to try to fall
asleep in a life raft. This is what it's like
to say goodnight and mean goodbye.

This Machine Kills Fascists

The irony of the Woody Guthrie Center
in Tulsa, Oklahoma is that it's financed
by oil barons. The Kaiser family helped build
things like the Hoover Dam. The Kaiser family
are probably made of gold. There's a "Woody Guthrie
Music Bar." The bathrooms are immaculate
and modern. Nothing is covered in dust. Everyone
in all the videos speaks with no accent, except
for Steve Earle, whose first word was probably
"Y'all." Woody was, you see,

not a great singer, painter, or even
guitarist, but Woody did not give a shit.
Woody drew cartoons despite having
no idea how to draw. To call Woody Guthrie
a hero is true despite the fact that
a hero is supposed to have muscles
and a destination in mind. If Woody

were alive today he would be a crust punk.
He would be both amazed and thankful
that people still ride the rails and that
there are still boxcars to ride in. He would have
a pitbull named Pete Seeger. Woody would
take one look at this museum and decide
he needs to sleep on the floor. He would
write some new songs on the walls. He would
discover spraypaint and spray on all
of his cans: This Machine Kills Fascists.

Dust Mop

This story requires some exposition, so here
goes: my friend, let's call her Mary

because her name actually is Mary,
works for Teach For America. She teaches

at Todd County Middle School
on the Rosebud Reservation

in South Dakota, and she has asked us,
us being me and my girlfriend, name given

upon request, to teach a poetry workshop
for her kids. Great. With that out of the way,

I would like to now say this. I have been
reading Sherman Alexie's poems for a few

years, and he talks a lot about how Indian
kids love basketball. I, being a good progressive

liberal socialist opponent of colonialism,
wanted to assume nothing about Indian kids

and basketball, but then they asked me to play
some five on five, so I will say that

these nine Indian kids can ball. Humility
is getting shook on by a 4'11" boy who is

eleven years your junior. I tore my shirt
trying to block Damante, and that is the extent

of what I have lost to Native Americans.

Song for Paula Deen

You are the Four Seasons or the Elvis
of food. Black folks have been doing this
for years, but put a white face on
it and suddenly all the butter won't

kill you. The butter, Paula. If no
butter send lard. If no lard
send fatback. Paula, I dream
of you, greased. I hold my hand
near your skin and find you are hot
enough. Did we do this to you or did you

want this to be done? I too have turned
food into sex and women into food, so come
on, Paula. Melt for me. Throw that hoecake
in the frier. Make me America
like I want you to want me to be.

OCD

The first time I saw her, everything
in my head went quiet. All the tics,
all the constantly refreshing images,
just disappeared. When you have

Obsessive Compulsive Disorder,
you don't really get quiet moments.
Even in bed I'm thinking

did I lock the door yes
did I wash my hands yes
did I lock the door yes
did I wash my hands yes.

But when I saw her, the only thing
I could think about was the hairpin curve
of her lips or the eyelash on her cheek

the eyelash on her cheek
the eyelash on her cheek.

I knew I had to talk to her.
I asked her out six times.
In thirty seconds. She said yes
after the third one, but none of them
felt right so I had to keep going.

On our first date, I spent more time
organizing my meal by color
than I did eating or talking to her,

but she loved it. She loved
that I had to kiss her goodbye
sixteen times, or twenty-four times

if it was Wednesday. She loved that
it took me forever to walk home
because there are a lot of cracks
in our sidewalk.

When we moved in together,
she said that she felt safe,
like no one would ever rob us
because I definitely locked the door
18 times. I'd always watch her mouth

when she talked when she talked when
she talked when she talked. When she

said she loved me, her mouth would curl up
at the edges. At night, she'd lay in bed
and watch me turn all the lights off and on

and off and on and off and on and off
and on and off. She'd close her eyes
and imagine that days and nights
were passing in front of her.

Some mornings, I'd start kissing her
goodbye but she'd just leave because
I was making her late for work.

When I stopped at a crack in the sidewalk,
she just kept walking. When she said
she loved me, her mouth was a straight line.

She told me I was taking up too much
of her time. Last week she started
sleeping at her mother's place.

She told me that she shouldn't
have let me get so attached to her,
that this whole thing was a mistake,
but how can it be a mistake

that I don't have to wash my hands
after I touch her? Love is not a mistake.
It's killing me that she can run away
from this and I just can't. I can't

go out and find someone new
because I always think of her.

Usually, when I obsess over things,
I see germs sneaking into my skin.
I see myself crushed by an endless
succession of cars. She was the first
beautiful thing I ever got stuck on.
I want to wake up every morning
thinking about the way she

holds her steering wheel. How she turns
shower knobs like she's opening a safe.
How she blows out candles blows out

candles blows out candles
blows out candles blows out
candles blows out candles
blows out—

now I just think about who else
is kissing her. I can't breathe because
he only kisses her once. He doesn't care
if it's perfect. I want her back so bad,

I leave the door unlocked.
I leave the lights on.

What the Cicadas Don't Understand

It's September. Don't you know, cicadas,
that it's September? The timing
is never right, cicadas. We never get to see
water becoming ice. Nothing

is ever right. If you fall asleep you always
wake up in the same place. You can
learn to sleep but that won't make you

a sleepwalker. You can learn to love
but that won't make you
a prisoner. You don't know

how to fix a bathtub drain, cicadas.
You run your finger
around the trap to clean out your long,
long hair, but every time

I tell you that, you don't listen,

you never listen,
cicadas. It's hard to hear music
when you are always making it. You can't
douse a fire and then

blame the ashes. You can't sing when it's cold,
cicadas. Steam, cicadas,
is the opposite of song, and remember
when I told you we never

get to see when water becomes steam?
We have to communicate,
cicadas. You have to tell me
what you need before everything

falls apart. Yes, you told me once.
You can't push once and watch something
fall over. Nothing changes just because
you want it to.

Moving Day

Today, as I was finishing the move
across town (and isn't it funny
how cliché, the literal catharsis
of throwing out all the things
I no longer need: my Seasonal
Affective Disorder lamp, all the
egg cartons, you know, for the project,
all of my ex-girlfriend's stuff
that survived the two previous purges:
curling iron, candles, painting
of her own face, swimsuit, bottle
opener, blender, all the now-dead
Christmas lights, all the food I can't save,
the chair, the older chair, the sheets
in which the bad thing happened, the things
in the bottom of the box that I will
try to landfill but will, as always, keep: the toy
my mother sent me that is just a squishy heart
filled with larvae, the bicycle
part I cannot identify, the handwriting
I also cannot identify, the sheets in which
the bad thing happened, the sugar
bowl, the sugar, the textbooks, the
instructions and signs and limits) a sparrow
flew just over my feet, its wings beating
against its own body, a sound not unlike
applause, and it hit the ground, and because
it was dead it lay still.

Little Poems

Everything You Ever Needed to Know about Silence

> You will never be more wrong than the first time
> you say "I love you." You will
> mean it, sure, but you'll still be lying.

I Didn't Recognize You without Your Glasses

> Though you chose to die five years ago, Alex,
> I still write your name on chalkboards
> and stray sheets of paper. I always
> leave out the E. I am not finished
> with you yet.

How to Kill Yourself without Hurting Anyone

> Don't.

Things that I Hope Are True about Heaven

> That the radio always plays
> what would have been your favorite
> songs. That there's always coffee
> if you want it. That you're
> there. That it's real.

Still Life with Pills

> I too have wanted to open myself. I too
> have stared at a razor and seen in it
> a doorway. I think I am only still here
> because I was too scared to make
> the first cut.

Clatter

> It is impossible to imagine a color
> you have not seen. Instead of dying,
> the jellyfish simply ceases
> to move. I complete five crosswords
> a day because it stops
> the panic. Trucks are downshifting
> on Main Street. Hair is partially
> composed of cyanide. Napalm
> is just gasoline and plastic. I am just
> carbon and bad timing.

The First Snow of the Year

> Alex, since I'm still here, I have to act
> as though I meant to be here. Once
> it snowed, and it wasn't that I felt
> great, because I felt awful, but awful
> is better than nothing. Depression wasn't
> an endless grey sky, it was no sky
> at all. I've got to go somewhere. I've got to go.

It Has Been and Will Be the Year of Airports

> I don't know where I will get
> the money, I don't know what
>
> I will tell my friends, I don't know how
> we will love each other in the nights of cold
>
> and quiet, but airplanes exist and will fly
> between where I live and where you are
>
> so hold on, I'm coming.

I Don't Know What "It" Is, But I Do Know where to Find It

> It's in the light sifting through your bedroom window.
> It's in the street when the whole world is pinched and slow.
> It's in the basement where you left it.
> It's in the ground. It's in your head.

Don't Give Up the Ship

> When the winds are picking up, when
> the sea around you turns from blue to grey,
> when the sky grows veins of light
> before you, let your arms become sails.
> Keep the lighthouse at your back.

I Cannot Answer You Tonight

> No one ever taught me how to pray,
> so I won't. Instead, I'll just say this:
> god bless the shape your head leaves
> in my pillow; god bless your insatiable
> hair; god bless you, though the hour is late,
> for you have come to me at last.

Parking Meter Theory

after Richard Siken and Paul Guest

That the coins become something other than coins
once the meter has eaten. Perhaps hamburger

patties. That we, therefore, are also
feeding the city. That the meters are a people

and that they are so very patient. That the credit
card-operated meters are an invasive species.

That we know not yet what we do. That parallel
parking is like making love but more difficult

and in public. That the curb is the border
of a great nation. Perhaps the curb is a shoreline.

Imagine one sidewalk as England and the other
sidewalk as France. Imagine parking meters

with longbows and trebuchets. Imagine
the poet imagining parking meters

in stupid metal hats. This is, laughably, considered
"work." Making glass is work. Driving a forklift

is work, as is procrastination, as is collecting coins
or lava or hamburgers, whichever they are.

Skyline with Cranes and Stormcloud

A broken clock is right twice a day, but there is no time
at which a broken windshield is useful. In my peripheral
vision, the cracks could be lightning, but Minneapolis
is not as interested in drama as I am. Somewhere, not here,

it is raining. It would be great if it would rain on me
because then there would be a reason I felt like garbage
right now. There's always, of course, a reason, but it would be
nice to say *It's raining only on my head* rather than

I have a chemical imbalance in my brain or *I just remembered
that someone I love will die before I do.* All of downtown
is underneath the sky. All of us stuck on the freeway
are underneath downtown and the sky. If you spend

long enough in one place you will eventually be hit
by lightning. Because it's not real lightning
we're discussing here, stay longer and you will
be hit twice. Never move, ever. You might go somewhere

there is no lightning. It might not rain there at all.

Our Numbered Days

Fun may often have little to no logical basis...
    Wikipedia

I never did a day's work in my life.
    Thomas Edison

*Writing stopped being fun when I discovered the difference
between good writing and bad and, even more terrifying, the
difference between it and true art.*
    Truman Capote

*In the past, some of the songs that were the most fun, and the
most entertaining and the most rocking, fell by the wayside
because I was concerned with what I was going to say and how I
was going to say it.*
    Bruce Springsteen

This suspense is terrible. I hope it will last.
    Oscar Wilde

*Now I am about to take my last voyage, a great leap into the
dark.*
    Thomas Hobbes

Mama, we came to dance.
    Brian Fallon

Fun as meditation, meditation being
doing exactly what you want to do
at the exact moment you want
to do it. When I say "I am having fun"
I am also saying "I can't imagine
being anywhere else." So suck it,

depression. I don't need you, I have
not needed you, and even when I don't
mean it I will say I'm having fun
and I don't want to be anywhere else.
I will wield my joy like a broadsword
or a fucking nerf gun. I will have
fun like my life depends on it
because it does.

On Sitting on My Ex-Girlfriend's Porch, Listening to Her Play a Song about Me that I Know Her New Boyfriend Helped Her Write

OK, babe, the fuck. I know you think
that art is all about openness
and total honesty, but honesty is like
an ugly puppy. I don't want it.

I know I should but I don't.
If you aren't going to put down
the ukulele and say "Remember
when I broke your heart and then I wrote

this song? I'm so happy that's in
the past. I'm so happy we're married,"
don't play the song. If you aren't
going to be the person the song

says you are, someone who believes
in permanence and redemption
and America, someone who, like,
loved me once, don't play the song.

I'm Sorry Your Kids Are Such Little Shits and that We Are in the Same Zen Garden

It's unfortunate that your offspring
make people wish for a dystopian future
in which euthanasia is a universally

beloved form of birth control, but when
elderly women literally everywhere are better
parents than you, perhaps it's time

to hang up the baby-making spurs. You are
to Japanese gardens what roosters are to the morning.
You are like golf: I hate you. I realize

that you have four children, all of whom
are particularly strong-willed, and that
you're tired, and that you might not

get the support you need from your wife,
but dude, your kids are being dicks to each other
loudly within earshot of me, and I'm gonna

throw them in this koi pond. Did you know
that koi are predatory? They're not, but I am smarter
than you, so let's pretend I'm right.

The News Anchor Is Crying

Because I called in during a Q and A
segment and broke up with her on air.

Q: Is dating a news anchor the dangerous
and sexy fun you would imagine?

A: I never got to ride in a helicopter. A: I never
got to see horrific tiger accidents. A: She never

took me tanning or teeth-bleaching. She also
never said "I love you," but that was probably

because A: she half-believes she is a robot
but with less emotional capacity, circuits

where the veins should be, or A: because the dark
is rising, or A: because her hair and thereby the timing

was never right, or A: because she actually didn't
love me, because she probably didn't, why

would she, but anyway, the news anchor is crying
and now she has to report on a shooting,

another shooting on the north side of town
and her hair is just right. The tears are just so.

Our Numbered Days

Depression is the inability to construct a future.
　　Rollo May

Sanity is a little box.
　　Charles Manson

He went out alone, and an hour and half later returned to announce, "I've had eighteen straight whiskeys. I think that's the record."
　　on the death of Dylan Thomas

I feel certain that I'm going mad again. I feel we can't go through another one of those terrible times. And I shan't recover this time. I begin to hear voices.
　　Virginia Woolf

You are always ticking inside me.
　　Sierra DeMulder

It is often suggested that creativity and bipolar disorder are linked.
　　Wikipedia

I put my heart and soul into my work, and have lost my mind in the process.
　　Van Gogh

The fishermen know that the sea is dangerous and the storm terrible, but they have never found these dangers sufficient reason for remaining ashore.
　　Van Gogh

I am concerned
that if I begin taking
medication I will no longer
be able to write poems.

Here and Away

I've been hearing that the world is ending.
I've heard it so much these days
that I can either completely ignore it
or never leave my house again.
That is, if I actually left my house
for things that don't directly enable
me to keep my house. See, I've been thinking
about driving nowhere. I've been thinking
about becoming a box inside a locked room
inside a dark house at the dark end of the street.
I wanna go away until I'm gone. It takes so much
less energy to not exist than it does to exist
and get burned. I've been burned so much
I'm not me anymore. I'm a stupid puppet version
of me. I've got strings that lead to nowhere.
Nothing is pulling on me. I wish someone
would drag my hand out of hiding
and sign my name on the dotted line.
There are days when I cannot find the sun
even though it's right outside my goddamn
window, when getting out of bed feels like the key
in the doomsday machine, so on those days,
this is what I tell myself: whatever
you are feeling right now, there is
a mathematical certainty that someone
is feeling that exact thing. This is not
to say you aren't special. This is to say
thank god you aren't special. I too
have kissed no one goodnight.
I have launched myself off tall places
and hoped no one would catch me.
I have ended relationships because suddenly
I was also exposed. But isolation is not safety,
it is death. If no one knows you're alive,
you aren't. If a tree falls in the forest
and no one's around to hear it, it does
make a sound, but then that sound is gone.
I am not saying you will find the meaning of life
in other people. I am saying that other people
are the life to which you provide the meaning.

See, we are wrong when we say I think,
therefore I am. The more we say it,
the more it sounds like, "I think,
therefore I will be." You cannot think yourself
into a full table. You cannot think and make
walls and a roof appear around you.
I have thought and thought myself into corners
made of words, nightmares, and what
has it gotten me but more thoughts,
a currency that only buys more currency.
So please, if you want to continue existing,
do something. Learn to make clouds with only
your breath. Build a house, even if every wall
leans to the left. Love it anyway, just like a season.
Just like a child. Love how you hate yourself sometimes,
because goddamn, at least there's still something
to hate. It's so easy to think and keep thinking
until you are the last person left on earth.
Until the entire world is no larger than the space
between your bed and the light switch,
but I hear the world is ending soon.
When we go, and we're all going to go,
I will be part of it.

Our Numbered Days

Hope is the feeling we have that the feeling we have is not permanent.
Mignon McLaughlin

Who hopes for what he already has?
Paul of Tarsus

The basis of optimism is sheer terror.
Oscar Wilde

He who has never hoped can never despair.
George Bernard Shaw

It's OK. It's OK. Come back to me. I'm not who I thought I'd be.
Kristian Hallbert

In reality, hope is the worst of all evils, because it prolongs man's torments.
Friedrich Nietzsche

If one has truly lost hope, one would not be on hand to say so.
Eric Bentley

There is nothing so well known as that we should not expect something for nothing—but we all do and call it Hope.
Edgar Howe

Hope is a thing I drag out of storage
when I am done thinking; hope answers
my phone; hope breaks my furniture
and helps me rebuild before the next
party; hope turns into more hope
unless it does not in which case
it turns into more or less less
than what I had hoped for; hope
sinks; hope drinks with me and against
me; hope is my ride home; hope is
asleep, I'm asleep, dear god, I can't
stop sleeping.

Traffic, Lightning, Gutter

Let me tell you what it's like
to ride a bicycle in a hurricane.
Let's say the wind is blowing
east. You live to the east now.
Let's say it's hailing because it does,
as you know, do this in hurricanes.
The rain does surprisingly
fall in sheets. More like
snakes. More like ghosts
of snakes. Ghosts of snakes
that are running away from
you. It's not that they don't
love you, more that they too
are trying to get dry. Let me
tell you what it's like to get
dry. You will feel like
you swam there through
Minneapolis or Detroit or
Bogota, whichever
is the place where right now
you sleep. You are a superhero
with a cape made of water. All doors
make all of us superheroes, but you
made that cape. You and the rain.

Enabling: a Love Song

for and after my grandmother

It's called kissing the bottle
because of the way your lips move. I seem
to recall that your lips moved like that

on me once, but I doubt either of us
would remember now. Now, after
the years and what I'm sure must be

several houses full of glass. I bet you could
fill all the places we've lived together
with all the bottles we've emptied together.

Bob, I know you never much liked drink. I think
you only drank so I didn't feel lonely
so you didn't feel lonely. I'm lonely

now, Bob. How's heaven, Bob? You must have
gone to heaven. You spent too much time
taking care of me to do anything

bad. Our children have to give me the wine now.
Our children, who you always kissed goodnight
with your mouth or whatever implements were

closer at hand. Bob, this Christmas all the other words
were gone but I could still say your name. Everyone noticed,
but no one would tell me where you'd gone. I knew

where you'd gone, but I still expected you to walk
in the door with Spotty, who I know is also dead,
but there are too many deaths now

to use them to accurately measure time. Bob,
I looked into Marilyn's eyes and asked
a question. Every word was your name. Even if

I could have said anything else, I wouldn't.
She wiped the mashed potatoes off my chin
and said "I know. We miss him too." Bob, that's it.

I miss you. I'd forgotten what it was like. Since
you came home from the ocean I'd never not been
near you. I may have been sad, but never lonely.

My liver should have taken me years ago. I should have
died before you. It's your name I want
on my lips when I get there. I need to

ask everyone I meet where you've gone.

American Revolution Trail, Charlotte, North Carolina, Winter

It seems strange to call this winter
when this morning I walked across
frozen cheesefruit and left my jacket

in the car on the way to the Minneapolis
airport, wait, let me explain cheesefruit:
fruit that is awful and smells

like cheese, next question. So here's what's up
with Charlotte: downtown looks
like the Emerald City had a baby

with Heaven. White and silver, all of it,
and I'm sure that they moved all
the homeless people somewhere, but I am

not from here and have the luxury, no,
privilege of not knowing that. I am just here
to perform poems for a bunch of college

students and the college is not asking me
to acknowledge anyone's humanity, the college is not
asking me to know anything more than I already

know, I'm leaving tomorrow anyway, so I won't.
It seems strange to call this winter when what I know
of winter is not white but grey. Strange when

everything here is beautiful and none of it's home.
I feel like I've spent my whole life in transit. Strange
when I should want to, but I don't want to, stop.

It Was the Day I First Fell out of a Window, or, It Was the Day we Vacuumed the Couch, or, It Was the Day We as a Family Took Spotty to the Veterinarian, or, It Was the Day, when Asked about Pizza, Everyone Said "Cheese," or, It Was the Day We Were Going to Take Out the Christmas Tree, and then It Was the Evening We Were All Candles Floating in the Woods, or It Was the Evening before We All Dreamed of Rabbits Slowly Becoming Snow; If Alcoholism is the Mutual Friend that Will Eventually Introduce our Family to One Another, I Would Still Take into me that Iced Buzzsaw, Grandma, I Would Still Leave that Engine Running

after Hieu Minh Nguyen

Liminality

The best way to get to heaven is to take it with you.
    Henry Drummond

Our headlights snake across
the West Texas highway.

Out here they've only got
two kinds of music on the radio:

Country and Western. Her hair
touches my shoulder in the wind.

The road signs say turn ahead.
We sing along to songs our parents

taught us. Turn ahead. Steep cliff.
Her finger is curled around my belt loop.

Steep cliff. Pay attention. The road
curves away from me, my voice crumples

as we clip the guardrail, our back
wheels lift skyward, the car spins,

flips, the sky and the riverbed
fight for supremacy, our headlights

kick into space. All of our clothes
float around us. Her blouse

blossoms like a supernova,
the change in her cup holders

forms constellations glinting
in front of our eyes. We are astronauts

coming back to earth. When the nickel
stars settle in the dust, we hang upside-down,

dangling like marionettes from our seatbelts.
We unbuckle them, fall to the ceiling

that was never meant to be a floor.
Her collarbone is broken, the same one

she fractured at six years old.
The glass is flung around the car

in a perfect halo orbit, we're freezing
in our own solar system.

As I'm blinking in and out
of consciousness, she speaks

to me in a voice that comes from
just behind my ear, she says:

"All that has ever mattered is volume
and if you turn up the speakers

past the point of sound, to deafening
silence, you will hear me again,

I will whisper your name
from the cracks in the canyon rocks

and you will know that this is heaven,
knowing that someone will always remember

your irises and where you hid your love
letters and why you could never speak

in anything but short sentences.
It's not a golden escalator

or a glowing choir conveying you
into the sky. The hand of God

does not reach down and pluck you
from your earthly shell, no,

the way to heaven is here, in your
last moments, these last half-seconds

before your soul shivers out of your bones.
You will see the candle on your first

birthday cake, the brush of your mother's
braids, smell your father's shaving cream

on the day he taught you there is a tornado
in your throat. You will hear our whispered

phone calls, our entwined *I love you*'s
and their softness will weigh down on you.

Heaven is an exhausted horse
laying down to die, it's you and your

ceiling fan conversing in whispers, Heaven
is floating to earth in this already-shattered car.

I will lie here forever and sing to you all the things
I stopped myself from saying when we were alive."

Acknowledgments

Thank you to the editors and staff of the publications in which the following poems, in various versions, have appeared:

Orange Quarterly: "Our Numbered Days"

Viral: "OCD"

I would like to thank Anny for always being my best friend; Sam, Dylan, Michael, and Riley for knowing where I need to be and what I need to be doing; my mother Marilyn for being the best mother; my brother Paden for being the best brother; Hieu for being the best Hieu; Ryan for being dope at producing my record; Sue and everyone at The College Agency for keeping me in shoes without holes; and everyone who has ever bought my books, listened to my poems, edited my poems, booked me for a show, or laughed at one of my stupid jokes. You are why this book is something you can hold in your hands.

About the Author

Neil Hilborn is a College National Poetry Slam champion, and a 2011 graduate with honors from Macalester College with a degree in Creative Writing. Neil was a member of the Macalester Poetry Slam team which ranked first at the 2011 College National Poetry Slam. He co-coached the 2012 Macalester team, leading them to a second place finish nationally. He was also a member of the Minneapolis adult National Poetry Slam team in 2011, which placed 5th out of 80 teams from cities across the country at the adult National Poetry Slam. He is the co-founder of *Thistle*, a Macalester literary magazine, and he runs writing workshops and performs at colleges and high schools around the country.

Other Books by Button Poetry

Aziza Barnes, *me Aunt Jemima and the nailgun.*

J. Scott Brownlee, *Highway or Belief*

Sam Sax, *A Guide to Undressing Your Monsters*

Nate Marshall, *Blood Percussion*

Mahogany L. Browne, *smudge*

Sierra DeMulder, *We Slept Here*

Danez Smith, *Black Movie*

Cameron Awkward-Rich, *Transit*

Jacqui Germain, *When the Ghosts Come Ashore*

Hanif Willis-Abdurraqib, *The Crown Ain't Worth Much*

Aaron Coleman, *St. Trigger*